Global Warming

by Bonnie Juettner

ERICKSON PRESS

Yankton, South Dakota

ERICKSON PRESS

LIBRARY OF CONGRESS CATALOGING-IN-PUBLICATION DATA

Juettner, Bonnie.
  Global warming / by Bonnie Juettner.
    p. cm. — (Ripped from the headlines)
  Includes bibliographical references and index.
Summary: This high-interest book for low-reading-level students discusses the causes and effects of global warming and whether action is needed to reduce its impact. Topics examined include theories about climate change, the effects of fossil fuels and greenhouse gases, carbon footprints, melting glaciers and rising sea levels, and animals at risk due to climate change.
  ISBN: 978-1-60217-024-7 (hardcover: alk. paper)
1. Global warming—Juvenile literature. I. Title.
  QC981.8.G56J84 2008
  363.738'74—dc22

                                                              2007045777

Printed in the United States of America

Contents

Melting Glaciers

Most people have never seen a glacier. A glacier is a frozen river of ice. It is a part of the ice that covered much of the world during the last ice age. Glaciers do not melt, even in the summer. So they are very old. Some glaciers are more than 100,000 years old. Some glaciers are very big. They can fill entire valleys. Other glaciers are smaller. Even though they are made of solid ice, glaciers can flow across land. But they flow very slowly. They may move only a few inches in a day.

In 1910, President William Howard Taft traveled to Montana to see one of America's greatest natural wonders. It was an area that contained 150 glaciers. President Taft made the area into a national park. The new park was named after its glaciers. It was called Glacier National Park.

Since the park was named, 90 percent of its ice has melted. "It's like watching the Statue of Liberty melt," says Daniel Fagre. Fagre is a geologist. A geologist is a scientist who studies Earth's crust. Part of

Walls of water flow from melting snow and ice in Glacier National Park.

Fagre's job is to hike out to glaciers and measure them. As the glaciers melt, his job is getting harder. The glaciers are getting smaller. So the edge of each glacier's ice is retreating. Fagre must hike farther each time in order to reach the edge of a glacier. "This glacier used to be closer,"[1] he remarks, as he heads toward Sperry Glacier.

Sperry Glacier has lost more than 500 acres (202 ha) of ice. It used to cover 800 acres (324 ha), but in 2004 it covered less than 250 (101 ha). It is one of the few glaciers that still exist in the park. Out of the original 150, only 30 are left. The glaciers that remain have lost two-thirds of their ice. Even those glaciers will be gone by 2030.

Like many other glaciers, Exit Glacier in Alaska is melting.

The glaciers are melting because of global warming. Global warming means that Earth's temperature is slowly rising. In some places, temperatures are rising enough to cause ice to melt.

People disagree about whether global warming will cause problems for life on Earth. Melting glaciers may cause floods. Some parts of Earth may become too hot and too dry. Global warming may also have some benefits. Warming may make it possible to farm in new areas. Some places that used to be too cold for farming may become able to support crops.

It is hard for anyone to predict the future. Scientists know that Earth is warming. But they do not know exactly how warm Earth will become. They do not know how fast temperatures will rise. They do not know which plants and animals will be able to change. And they are not sure which plants and animals will become extinct. (When a plant or animal becomes extinct, it means that there are no living members of its species left on Earth.) Because scientists do not know the answers to these questions, they cannot be sure exactly how global warming will affect Earth and its people.

Chapter 1

How Real Is the Threat of Global Warming?

I n 1880 Earth's temperature was 57°F (14°C). In 2004 it was 58°F (15°C). Earth's temperature has risen by one degree. That does not sound like very much. One degree is not enough to cause glaciers to melt, unless the change is from just below freezing to just above freezing.

However, scientists say that 6,000 years ago, North America was covered with forests. But then Earth's climate changed. Earth's temperature went up 2 to 4°F (1 to 2°C). And North America's plant life shifted. Land that was once covered by forest became grassland. America's Great Plains formed. How could such a small change in temperature cause such a large change in the land?

Average Temperatures

Earth's temperature is only an average. Earth is not the same temperature all over. Some places are hotter. Some are colder. The average is a number in the middle. If the average increase in temperature is one degree, this means that some parts of Earth are warming up much more than one degree. For example, temperatures near the Arctic Circle are rising ten times as fast as temperatures in the rest of the world. Greenland's winter temperature has gone up much more than one degree. It has gone up 9°F (5°C).

At the same time, other parts of Earth are getting cooler. The southeastern United States has more clouds than it used to. So it is getting a little cooler. But because Earth's average temperature has gone up

Figuring Average Temperatures

Imagine the weather for one day on Earth. It might be below freezing in McGrath, Alaska. It could be hot and sunny in Deming, New Mexico. It could be rainy and cool in New York City. Its temperature is different everywhere.

It is possible to figure out Earth's average temperature. First, scientists collect thousands of temperatures. They gather data from all over the world. They make a list. Then they find the temperature that is exactly in the middle. This temperature is Earth's average for the day.

Some scientists say that Earth's temperature means nothing. It does not explain what the weather is like in any one place. Other scientists feel that an average temperature is important. It is a way to explain how Earth is changing overall.

a degree, scientists say that Earth is experiencing global warming. People living in cooling areas may not notice the change. But near the poles, temperatures have gone up enough to make ice start to melt.

The Greenhouse Effect

Earth would not be warm at all, not even warm enough to support life, if it were not for the greenhouse effect. The greenhouse effect allows Earth to trap heat from the Sun. A greenhouse is a small house built of glass or clear plastic. It traps heat from sunlight. This is like what happens when a car is parked in the sun. Light and heat can enter the car through the glass windows. Heat from the Sun gets trapped inside the car. The temperature in the car is much warmer than the temperature outside. A greenhouse stays even warmer than the inside of a car. A greenhouse will stay warm even in the winter. Plants can grow inside it even when snow is on the ground outside.

Earth has something that can act like the glass walls of a greenhouse. Earth has an atmosphere. The atmosphere contains all the gases that make up Earth's air. Planets that have no atmosphere cannot trap heat from the Sun. Instead, they reflect most of the Sun's heat back into space. Earth's atmosphere, though, traps some of the Sun's heat. For this reason, Earth stays much warmer than the temperature in space. Space is very cold.

The Greenhouse Effect

Natural and manmade gases in Earth's atmosphere trap some of the heat from the Sun. To keep Earth's temperature constant, the balance of these gases must remain stable.

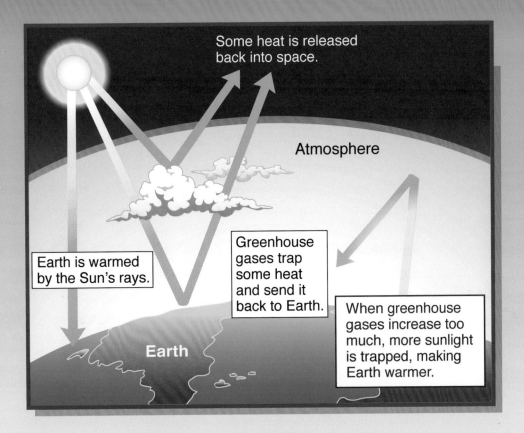

Some heat is released back into space.

Atmosphere

Earth is warmed by the Sun's rays.

Greenhouse gases trap some heat and send it back to Earth.

When greenhouse gases increase too much, more sunlight is trapped, making Earth warmer.

Earth

The Main Greenhouse Gases

Carbon dioxide:	Created when people and animals breathe
Methane:	Produced by cattle when they digest food
Nitrous oxide:	Comes from plants when they die and rot
Ozone:	Occurs naturally in the atmosphere
Water vapor:	Occurs naturally in the atmosphere

Source: http://www.ace.mmu.ac.uk/kids/globalwarming.html.

Earth is warmed by light from the Sun. But the Sun is 92 million miles (148 million km) away. If Earth had no atmosphere, the Sun's light would only warm Earth up to around 0°F (-18°C). Earth would be colder near the poles. It would be warmer near the equator. But it would still not be warm enough to support life. The greenhouse effect raises Earth's temperature more than 55°F (30°C). It makes Earth warm enough for humans.

Too Much Heat?

Plants and animals need Earth's greenhouse effect. But scientists believe the greenhouse effect is increasing. Earth's atmosphere has always trapped some heat. It also reflects some heat back into space. Now the atmosphere is trapping more heat than it used to. It is reflecting less heat into space. So Earth is getting warmer.

Rising temperatures could harm frogs and other animals.

Whether warmer temperatures are a threat to humans is a problem scientists want to answer. Scientists know that many plants and animals will become extinct. They also know that some plants and animals will be able to change. For example, some plants may spread to areas where they never used to grow. But scientists do not yet know exactly how humans will be affected.

Earth's Changing Climate

Scientists cannot predict exactly how much Earth's climate will change. But they are trying. To predict climate changes, scientists use computers. They collect data, or information. Then they build a computer program called a model. It shows events that can happen in the real world. For example, scientists have made computer models of hurricanes. They use these models to predict where hurricanes will strike. The models can also predict how strong a storm will be. They can also predict how much damage a hurricane will do if it hits a city.

Computer models can be complex. NASA is the National Aeronautics and Space Administration. It is the space agency for the U.S. government. NASA researches space. It works on finding ways to explore space. To do this, NASA uses many tools. One tool it uses is computer models. NASA's computers can make a model of Earth. They divide the atmosphere into ten layers. Then they divide each layer into

NASA uses these huge computers to predict changes in climate.

points. There are 650,000 points. The computers can calculate how a change would affect each point. To do this, the computers must make 80 million calculations every hour.

However, even NASA's computers cannot keep track of everything. There are too many different pieces, called variables. A variable is anything that can vary, or change. The temperature of ocean water is one variable. Warm water can speed a hurricane up. It can make the hurricane more intense. But hurricanes travel for hundreds of miles. The water temperature is not the same everywhere. Physical obstacles are also variables. Sandbars are a variable, for example. They can slow a hurricane down. And a

Stronger Hurricanes?

In 2005 three big hurricanes hit the United States. Their names were Katrina, Wilma, and Rita. All were category 5 storms. Category 5 storms are the strongest hurricanes. They can take the roofs off homes. Some have a deadly storm surge. A storm surge is a rush of water. It is above normal tide levels. Category 5 storm surges can be more than 18 feet (5.5m) tall.

The 2005 hurricanes broke several records. Katrina was the most destructive hurricane ever to hit the United States. Wilma was the most powerful storm ever in the Atlantic.

Scientists do not know whether global warming was to blame. Surface water in tropical oceans has gotten warmer. But it has warmed up less than half a degree. Scientists checked their computer models. Hurricanes should not be affected much by such a small change. They should be only about 2 percent stronger. But this time the models were wrong. Scientists have checked the data going back to 1950. Hurricanes have doubled in strength since then. In the last 30 years, the number of category 4 and category 5 hurricanes has also doubled.

But hurricanes have gotten worse only in the Atlantic. Storms in other oceans are no stronger. Scientists think the Atlantic Ocean is affected more by warming because it is a colder ocean. Global warming affects the whole Earth. But it affects different places differently.

hurricane is just one event. Earth's climate includes all the weather all over the world. Every storm is affected by hundreds of different variables. Even the formation of one cloud depends on many variables.

Garbage In, Garbage Out

The computers at NASA are very good. A really good computer can keep track of thousands of different variables. But a computer's model is only as good as the data it is based on. Good data includes a lot of information. The information is about many variables. When scientists have good data, their models can make good predictions. When they have less data, the models are more likely to be wrong. Scientists call this "garbage in, garbage out." If data is incorrect, it is "garbage." A model based on "garbage" data will be "garbage," too. On the other hand, if the data is good, the model should be, too.

Computers can keep track of many variables that affect climate. But they are missing some data. Today, scientists have many tools for collecting data. Satellites can collect weather data. And weather stations all over the world collect information. But people have only been collecting data about the weather for about 100 years. Scientists have some information about weather in ancient times. But they have to construct that data themselves from clues. Data about ancient weather is not very good. The data that is collected by modern tools today is

more accurate. Scientists know they do not have enough data. So they cannot be sure that their computer models are correct.

Mistaken Models

Scientists do know that their old computer models were partly correct. Computer models made in the late 1900s were not perfect. But they correctly predicted that Earth would get warmer. They predicted that glaciers would melt. The models were wrong about one thing. They did not get the speed of global warming exactly right. They did not predict that the ice would melt so fast.

The models did predict that sea ice in the Arctic Ocean would melt. They predicted that in the 21st century, it would become possible for ships to travel through the Arctic Ocean. It might not be possible all year. But it would be possible in the summer. They estimated that this would be possible by the year 2040.

In the summer of 2007, though, scientists realized that their models must have left something out. Ice was melting fast. It was melting much faster than the models had predicted. Every summer, some ice melts in the Arctic. It freezes again in the winter. But in the summer of 2007, far more ice melted than usual. It opened up 1 million square miles (2.6 million sq. km) of water that would normally have stayed

Water flows down
a melting iceberg.

frozen. So much ice melted that an ice-free passage through the Arctic Ocean opened up. It was 33 years ahead of schedule. Scientists scrambled to redo their computer models. Now the models predict an ice-free Arctic Ocean by 2013.

A Model for Antarctica

Now scientists are trying to make a model that will predict Antarctica's climate. But this is hard. Antarctica is large. It is about as big as the United States and Mexico combined. North America has thousands of weather stations that record changing temperatures. Antarctica has only 100. And Antarctica's weather stations have only been there for 50 years.

With so little data, it is hard for computer models to predict what will happen. Scientists have made models anyway. So far, the models have been only partly right. The models have shown that Antarctica would warm up quickly. Antarctica is warming. But unlike the Arctic, the Antarctic is warming more slowly than the models predicted.

It is hard to predict how Earth's climate will change. There is a lot of debate about what will happen. Even scientists disagree. They are not sure how fast Earth will warm. They do not know how much Earth will change because of the warming. But they do agree on one thing. The overall trend shown in the computer models is correct. Only the speed is wrong. Faster than anyone thought it would, Earth is getting warmer.

Chapter 2

What Causes Global Warming?

Weather changes every day. It may rain one day and be sunny the next. Climate is the weather for a long period. Like weather, climate can change. But climate changes normally happen over a long period of time. Climate does not normally change very much within a lifetime.

Earth and Its Orbit

Changes in the weather are part of nature. For example, the weather changes with the seasons. Winters are colder and summers are warmer. Seasonal changes are caused by Earth's tilt. Earth travels through space in a tilted position. Sometimes the North Pole is tilted toward the Sun. Then the Northern Hemisphere has summer weather. Other times the South Pole is tilted toward the Sun. Then the Southern Hemisphere has summer weather.

Earth's orbit around the Sun can also change Earth's climate. Earth's orbit around the Sun is an ellipse. Scientists calculate that Earth's orbit gets a little longer every 100,000 years. Then Earth travels farther from the Sun. Scientists have found that Earth's major ice ages happen when Earth's orbit carries Earth far from the Sun. An ice age is a period of time when Earth's temperatures drop. Ice sheets cover much of the land.

Ice ages are also affected by Earth's tilt. Like Earth's orbit, Earth's tilt is not always the same. It alternates between 22° and 24°. It takes 41,000 years for Earth's tilt to shift from 22° to 24°. Earth's tilt change starts a cold period every 41,000 years. Earth also wobbles on its axis. It wobbles as if it were a spinning top. But Earth is much larger than a top. It wobbles more slowly. Every 19,000 to 23,000 years, Earth wobbles in a way that tilts it a little farther from the Sun. When this happens, Earth also gets colder. And when Earth wobbles back, it warms up again.

Changes in the Sun

Changes in Earth's climate can also be caused by the Sun. Sometimes the Sun changes. It may give off more heat. Or it may give off a little less heat. Scientists at NASA have studied Earth's last ice age, the Little Ice Age. The Little Ice Age occurred from the 1400s to the 1700s. The coldest part was from 1645 to 1715. It was not a true ice age. It was not cold enough to cover Earth with ice sheets. But it was cold enough to make it impossible to travel to Greenland or Iceland by ship. And it caused canals in the Netherlands to freeze solid.

The Tilt of the Earth and the Seasons

Seasons change because of the tilt of the Earth. This tilt causes the Sun to shine more directly on different parts of Earth during the year, making the seasons change.

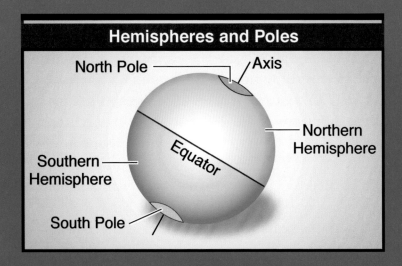

Hemispheres and Poles

- North Pole
- Axis
- Northern Hemisphere
- Equator
- Southern Hemisphere
- South Pole

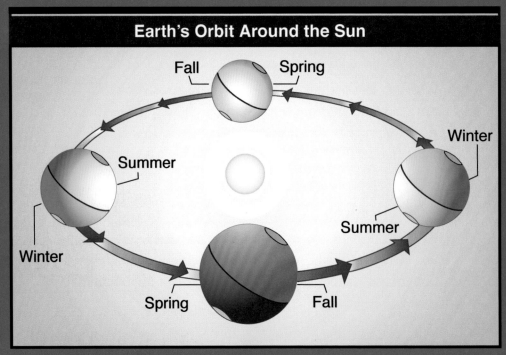

Earth's Orbit Around the Sun

- Fall
- Spring
- Winter
- Summer
- Winter
- Summer
- Spring
- Fall

Source: http://gpc.edu/~pgore/Earth&Space/GPS/seasons.html.

Scientists think the Sun was dimmer during the Little Ice Age. During the Little Ice Age, Galileo discovered sun spots. He and other scientists made charts of the Sun's spots. The charts show that the Sun only had about 50 spots in 30 years. Normally, the Sun would have 40,000 or 50,000 spots during that amount of time. Scientists think that the Sun gave off less energy during this time. It warmed Earth less than usual. After 1715 the Sun began to give off more energy. Sun spots appeared more often. The Little Ice Age slowly began to draw to a close. By around 1800 the Little Ice Age was over.

Sun spots, shown here in red, were charted by Galileo long ago.

Industrial Revolution

The Industrial Revolution began around 1800. The Little Ice Age was just ending. Humans began to build factories. For the first time, machines could make things. For example, machines could make clothing. Many people stopped making their own

Clues from Earth's Past

Scientists have been recording Earth's temperature for more than 100 years. That may seem like a long time. But Earth is nearly 4 billion years old. Scientists must look for clues to figure out what the Earth's temperature was so long ago.

One clue lies deep inside ice. Some of Greenland's ice is 120,000 years old. It froze before the last major ice age began. Antarctica's ice is even older. Some Antarctic ice is about 750,000 years old.

Scientists have studied samples of this ancient ice. They can tell how temperatures changed over the years. They can also tell what gases were in the air when each layer of ice formed. They find and study air bubbles in the ice. For example, they can tell how much carbon dioxide was in the air. Scientists wanted to know what the air was like before the Industrial Revolution. They found out that the amount of carbon dioxide in the air then was about 280 parts per million. It reached almost 384 parts per million in 2007.

A scientist in Iceland inspects an ice core sample.

clothes by hand. People began to buy things that were made from machines. People used to live and work mostly on farms. But now many people moved to cities. They found work in factories. Cities grew larger.

Machines need energy in order to run. During the Industrial Revolution, inventors found ways to provide energy. They started by burning coal. They could use energy from coal to make electricity. Then they could heat water and make steam. Inventors found ways to use steam power as a form of transportation. Railroads and steamships were invented. Later, inventors found ways to use oil. Like coal, oil is another fossil fuel. People began using oil to heat houses. They also used it in lamps. In the early

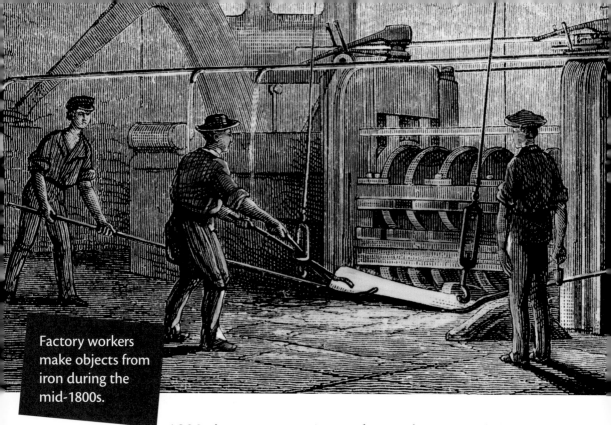

Factory workers make objects from iron during the mid-1800s.

1900s inventors starting making oil into gasoline. Gasoline can be used as fuel. Cars and trucks run on gasoline. Later they found ways to make gasoline that could be used in airplanes, helicopters, and even space shuttles.

Fossil Fuels and Global Warming

When the Industrial Revolution began, Earth was beginning to warm up. Earth was coming out of the Little Ice Age. But most scientists believe that the Industrial Revolution caused Earth to warm up even faster.

When a substance burns, it breaks down into other substances. When coal and oil burn, they give off carbon dioxide gas. The gas is released into the air. Carbon dioxide is a common gas on Earth. It is the same gas that humans exhale when they breathe. But it is also a greenhouse gas.

Greenhouse Gases

Greenhouse gases add to the greenhouse effect. Not all the gases in Earth's atmosphere are greenhouse gases. The two most common gases are nitrogen and oxygen. But they are not greenhouse gases. Oxygen is a gas that people and animals need to breathe. It is also a gas that plants release into the air.

Greenhouse gases can trap heat close to Earth's surface. The two most important greenhouse gases are carbon dioxide and water vapor. Earth always has both these gases in its air. Water cycles between land, oceans, and the sky. Carbon does, too. Normally, carbon is stored in plants, animals, and the oceans. Animals breathe out carbon dioxide. It is also released when plant or animal matter starts to rot.

Carbon dioxide is part of nature. It is always in the air. It would be in the air even if people never burned fossil fuels. Every year carbon dioxide cycles between plants and the air. Even more cycles between the air and the oceans. About 60 billion tons (54 billion t) cycles between plants and the air. Another 90 billion tons (80 billion t) of carbon dioxide cycle between the air and the oceans.

However, when people burn coal, gas, and oil, they add even more carbon dioxide to the air. Humans add 5 or 6 billion tons (4.5 or 5.4 billion t)

Other Greenhouse Gases

Carbon dioxide and water vapor are the two most important greenhouse gases. But they are not the only ones. Other greenhouse gases also add to global warming.

Methane is a greenhouse gas that exists in nature. Methane is produced when plant or animal matter rots. Natural gas is mostly methane. Burning natural gas adds methane to the air. Landfills also add methane to the air. Rotting garbage gives off methane. So does sewage. About 9 percent of greenhouse gases given off by human actions are methane. Methane can trap about 100 times as much heat as carbon dioxide can. But it does not stay in the air for as long. It remains in the air for about ten years.

Nitrous oxide is another greenhouse gas. It also exists in nature. It is sometimes called laughing gas. It is used by dentists to help patients relax. But dentists are not the main source of nitrous oxide in the air. Farmers are. Many farmers use fertilizers to help their crops grow. Chemical fertilizers often contain nitrous oxide.

Humans also make some greenhouse gases that do not exist in nature. One kind are chlorofluorocarbons. They are also called CFCs. CFCs were once used in aerosol cans. They were also used in air conditioners. They are not used much anymore. Most American companies have stopped making them. But CFCs can remain in the air for 100 years.

Experts worry about carbon dioxide coming from factories and other sources.

of carbon dioxide to the air every year. That carbon dioxide will stay in the air for more than 100 years. So every year the amount in the air rises. The level of carbon dioxide in the air has increased by about 25 percent since 1900.

In 1958 scientists began to wonder about carbon dioxide. They started to carefully measure its levels in the air. They tested the air at Mauna Loa, Hawaii. They measured in parts per million. Parts per million is the number of parts of a gas in a million molecules of air. Scientists estimated carbon dioxide levels for the year 1800. Then, a million molecules of air probably contained 280 parts of carbon dioxide. In 1958 a million molecules of air contained 315 parts of carbon dioxide. In 1995 a million molecules of air contained 361 parts of carbon dioxide.

The moss in this fossil grew 20 million years ago when the Earth was warmer.

Carbon dioxide levels slowly rose. And Earth slowly got warmer.

It has been thousands of years since the last time Earth had so much carbon dioxide in its atmosphere. Some scientists think it has been at least 20 million years. Twenty million years ago the Earth was in the early Miocene period. The climate was much warmer than it is today. Palm trees grew in England. As Earth grew warmer, some forests were replaced with grasslands.

Are Both Sides Right?

Scientists and politicians disagree about the causes of global warming. Some people believe that adding carbon dioxide to the air is not important. They think that Earth's warming is caused by changes in Earth's orbit. They also think warming might be caused by changes in the Sun. They feel the changes that helped stop the Little Ice Age are still progressing.

Some scientists hypothesize that carbon dioxide levels rise naturally. They think this might happen whenever the planet gets warmer. They say that carbon dioxide levels may rise after the planet warms. The changes might be an effect, not a cause, of warming.

Can both sides be right? In this case, they can. In fact, scientists on both sides of this issue agree on most of the facts. They agree that Earth is getting much warmer. They agree that changes in climate are a natural part of Earth's history. They also agree that humans add carbon dioxide to the air. They agree that burning fossil fuels increases the amount of carbon dioxide in the air. And they agree that carbon dioxide is a greenhouse gas that can cause warming.

It is likely that both sides are right. Earth would still be getting warmer even if the Industrial Revolution had never occurred. In that case, Earth would warm much more slowly. Burning fossil fuels speeds up the warming process. But how will global warming affect life on Earth?

Chapter 3

What Will Be the Effects of Global Warming?

Earth has been through vast climate changes in the past. Dinosaurs lived during one of Earth's warmest times. One of these times was the Cretaceous period. Earth was mostly warm and wet. No ice covered the North and South Poles. Most lowlands were covered by shallow seas. Recently, scientists discovered that Earth's oceans were hot during this time. In some areas the Atlantic Ocean was as warm as a hot tub.

Scientists hope that Earth will not become as warm as it was during the Cretaceous period. When dinosaurs were alive, greenhouse gas levels were much higher than they are today. The air included vast amounts of carbon dioxide. Levels were between 1,300 and 2,300 parts per million. Today carbon dioxide in the air is increasing. But in 2007 it was still only 384 parts per million.

Shrinking Sea Ice

Scientists cannot predict the future. But they can document the changes that are already happening.

Many of these changes are occurring near the poles. Earth's polar regions, the Arctic and Antarctic, are warming much faster than the rest of the world. Arctic Ocean ice has been decreasing at the rate of 8 percent every year. So far it has lost 540,000 square miles (1.4 million sq. km) of ice. That is an area twice the size of Texas.

Soon the Arctic Ocean may be entirely free of ice. Ships have already been able to travel in the Arctic without using icebreakers. In the future the Arctic Ocean may be used as a shipping route. If so, port cities may spring up along the northern coasts of

Dinosaurs lived on Earth during a very warm period.

The Arctic: How Warm Could It Get?

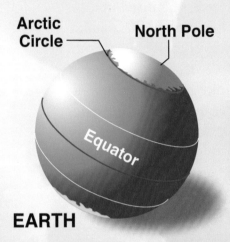

Arctic Circle — **North Pole**

Equator

EARTH

The frigid Arctic is warming more quickly than the rest of the world. Some experts say temperatures in the region may increase several degrees by the middle of the 21st century.

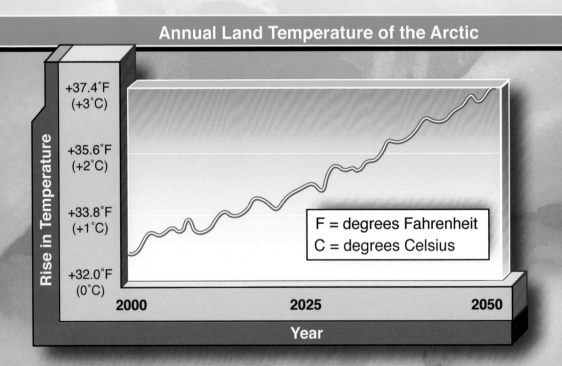

Annual Land Temperature of the Arctic

Rise in Temperature

+37.4°F (+3°C)

+35.6°F (+2°C)

+33.8°F (+1°C)

+32.0°F (0°C)

F = degrees Fahrenheit
C = degrees Celsius

2000   2025   2050

Year

Source: Hugo Ahlenius, UNEP/GRID-Arendal, Projected Temperatures in the 21st Century, UNEP/GRID-Arendal Maps and Graphics Library, http://maps.grida.no/go/graphic/projected-temperatures-in-the-21th-century / Sources: Wang, M., Overland, J.E., Kattsov, V., Walsh, J.E., Zhang, X, and Pavlova, T. (2007). Intrinsic versus forced variation in coupled climate model simulations over the Arctic during the 20th century. *J. Climate,* 20(6), 1093-1107.

Europe, Asia, and North America. Oil companies hope to find more oil buried under the Arctic Ocean. The United States, Russia, Canada, Norway, and Denmark all have claimed parts of the Arctic Ocean. They want the rights to any oil that is found within their borders.

Like the Arctic, Antarctica is losing ice. In 2002 Antarctica's Larsen B ice shelf broke up and fell into the sea. It was larger than the state of Rhode Island. It was about 12,000 years old. The ice shelf was located on the Antarctic Peninsula. This part of Antarctica is "one of the most rapidly warming parts of Earth,"[2] says David Bromwich. Bromwich is a scientist who studies polar climates. The Antarctic Peninsula is warming about 10 times faster than the rest of the world. All in all, Antarctica loses about 59 square miles (153 sq. km) of ice each year.

However, Antarctica as a whole is not losing ice as fast as the Arctic. That is because most of Antarctica is not warming yet. The Antarctic Peninsula is warmed by sea currents. But Antarctica's interior is still frozen solid. "It's hard to see a global warming signal from the mainland of Antarctica right now,"[3] remarked David Bromwich in 2007.

Rising Sea Levels

As ice in the Arctic and Antarctic melts, it turns to water. Then it runs into the ocean. If enough ice melts, it could cause sea levels to rise.

Even if ice were not melting, sea levels would still rise. In fact, sea levels have been rising for years. For

A Nation Lost?

Global warming affects some regions, especially Earth's poles, more than others. Sea level rise affects different areas differently, too. Tuvalu is a country made up of nine islands. It is located in the Pacific Ocean. In Tuvalu the sea is rising almost a quarter of an inch (5.5mm) every year.

Tuvalu's islands are made of coral. Coral is hollow. A sea wall cannot protect Tuvalu from the rising water. The water rushes in through the coral. It pushes its way up. Most people in Tuvalu live on Funafuti Atoll. There it floods twice a month. When it floods people gather around the airstrip. The airstrip is the highest point on the island. It is 12 feet (4m) above sea level. The highest flood so far has reached 11.5 feet (3.5m) above sea level. Most of the houses in Tuvalu are on stilts. But the flood water still seeped into the first floor of many people's homes.

The government of Tuvalu fears that one day, the whole country may flood. The people may have to flee. The people of Tuvalu hope that if this happens, they can migrate. They hope to move to Australia or New Zealand.

most of the 20th century, sea levels rose about a tenth of an inch (nearly 2mm) every year. However, this number is an average. Sea levels in some places rise more than others. For example, sea levels in San Diego and San Francisco have risen 7 inches (18cm) in the last century.

Now sea levels are rising a little faster. They are rising at the rate of 0.12 inches (3mm) a year. Part of the rise is due to ice melting. The rest is caused by warming oceans. When water gets warmer, it takes up more space. So when ocean water is warmer, the entire ocean takes up more space. Tides come in farther up the beach.

Scientists cannot be sure how much sea levels will rise in the future. Some think that sea levels will rise at least 8 inches (20cm) by 2100. In some places sea levels may rise even more. Scientists expect the sea level around New York City to rise at least 12 inches (30cm) by the 2080s. This would be enough to

Seawater swamps Funafuti Atoll at high tide.

shut down the New York City subway system. It would also flood many neighborhoods. In low-lying coastal lands, a sea level rise of just 1 foot (30cm) could flood 100 feet (30m) of land. Much of Florida, Louisiana, and California would be flooded.

Although it is not known how much sea levels will rise, some scientists think that many homes near the sea will be ruined. They are especially worried about homes that lie within 500 feet (just over 150m) of the ocean. By 2060, experts say, one quarter of those homes will be destroyed.

Loss of Coastline

Some Americans are already losing their homes. Flooding is not the only way that towns can lose land. In the Arctic, many communities rely on sea ice to protect their land. Open water can cause land to erode, or wear away. The water can carry away grains of sand and dirt. When the water is frozen for much of the year, the ice protects the land from eroding. Now that there is less sea ice, some northern coastal villages are losing ground. The water is eroding the land away from under their homes.

The Alaskan village of Shishmaref lies on an island off the coast of southwest Alaska. It will not be there very much longer. The village is losing 3 to 5 feet (0.91 to 1.52m) of land every year to erosion. Sometimes it loses more land than that to a single storm. Some storms have taken as much as 125 feet (38m) from the village. The 600 people who live in Shishmaref have decided to move. They

A man walks in the spot where his house once stood in the Alaskan village of Shishmaref.

will move to the mainland of Alaska. They hope to move by 2012.

Shishmaref is not the only coastal town to face this problem. In Alaska about 20 towns are considering moving. Almost 200 have problems with flooding and erosion.

Penguins at Risk

Like coastal towns, coastal animals are at risk. Animals in the Arctic and the Antarctic rely on sea ice. For example, the Adélie penguins live on the Antarctic Peninsula. They need sea ice. Without it, they are in danger.

Algae grows on sea ice. Krill feed on the algae. (Krill are sea animals, similar to shrimp.) The Adélie

penguins eat mostly krill. Less ice means fewer krill. The krill that survive are smaller. So penguins have less to eat. Lately, sea ice has disappeared for several years. In those years there is no algae. And there are fewer krill. Penguins can also eat fish. But in recent years, fish populations have dropped as well. As a result, fewer penguin chicks survive to become adults.

The Adélie penguins have another problem. Temperatures on the Antarctic Peninsula have warmed so much that sometimes it rains. The rain makes it hard for penguins to keep their eggs warm.

Even the snow that falls may melt quickly. Science writer Meredith Hooper went to Antarctica to see the penguins. She writes: "If birds stand up to shift position, snow falls on the eggs to melt into a puddle. Eggs are crushed or kicked out of nests as birds

Signs of Early Spring

Summer is getting longer. Spring comes early. Autumn begins late. Some scientists are saying that March 21 is not the first day of spring in North America anymore. Now spring begins around March 13. The growing season for plants lasts thirteen days longer than it used to.

When spring starts early, insects come out early, too. For example, in Spain butterflies are coming out eleven days earlier than they used to. Birds that stay in Spain all winter are not bothered by this change. They realize that spring has begun. But for birds that migrate south for the winter, this is a problem. These birds are still returning to Spain at about the same time as always. These birds rely on caterpillars as a food source. But if the caterpillars come out and spin their cocoons early, then the birds arrive after the caterpillars are gone. By then the caterpillars have all become butterflies. This means that birds do not get as much food to eat. They do not lay as many eggs. Slowly, the number of birds that migrate to Spain is dropping.

When birds do not eat the insects, more of them survive. They lay more eggs. Those eggs hatch. As a result, there are more insects later in the summer than there usually would be.

try to deal with the snow. Or the eggs lie cold, flooded out. . . . Cold doesn't affect the chicks. It's the rain, soaking their down, forcing them to shiver, using up vital calories in an attempt to keep warm."[4]

In the last 30 years, the Adélie penguin population has declined. There are 30 percent fewer penguins than before. Eventually, they may not be able to survive anywhere on Earth.

The Adélie are not the only penguins in danger. Penguins also live at the southern tips of Africa and South America and on some islands in the southern Indian Ocean. Warmer seas also reduce their food supply. Seas that are even a fraction of a degree warmer than they used to be can reduce penguin survival rates by 10 percent.

Polar Bears Facing Extinction

Polar bears face the same problem. Polar bears do not eat algae or krill. But they do eat seals. To get to the seals, they travel along the sea ice. Between ice flows, they swim. Polar bears are strong swimmers. It is not hard for them to swim 15 miles (24km). But now the ice is breaking up. Sometimes polar bears must swim as far as 60 miles (96km). Such long distances are challenging even for good swimmers. Many polar bears cannot make it that far. They drown instead.

Another problem for polar bears is that winter ice is breaking up earlier in the spring. Ice is breaking up about three weeks early. Polar bears used to be able to feed on seal pups during those weeks. They

put on weight during that time. Now that the ice is breaking up earlier, polar bears weigh less. In one part of Canada, polar bears weigh 150 pounds (68kg) less than they did 30 years ago. Some bears are having a very hard time finding food. They have started to raid village garbage dumps.

Scientists say that in 50 years, polar bears will not exist in Alaska or Russia. A few polar bears may survive in Canada and Greenland. "As the sea ice goes, so goes the polar bear,"[5] says Steve Amstrup. Amstrup is a scientist who studies the Arctic.

Changes in Farming

Just as polar bears depend on sea ice, farmers depend on weather. Most scientists expect global warming to have a strong effect on farmers. In North America, warming has already made the growing season longer. Spring begins about a week earlier. That means that farmers can plant crops earlier.

Meanwhile, scientists are finding it harder to predict the weather. They think that storms will be more fierce. But they also think that droughts and forest fires will last longer. Both storms and droughts can destroy crops. Climate expert Jim Salinger explains: "As you heat up the atmosphere, it rains harder when it rains. But when it doesn't, things dry out faster because it's hotter. You get more flooding *and* more drought."[6]

Exactly how warming affects each farm, though, depends on where the farm is located. Global warming should cause some areas to get more rain. More rain could make it easier to grow some crops. But it could also lead to flooding. In 2007 rain destroyed crops in western India. Floods killed hundreds of people. Some people blamed global warming. But others insisted that storms have always been fierce during India's rainy season.

At the same time, other areas could experience dry spells and droughts. Some fertile areas will turn

A farmer works his crops. Growing seasons are getting longer in some places.

into desert. For example, the Sahara Desert is already spreading. So is the desert of northern China. In China killer dust storms, called the "black wind," have become common. The desert is spreading toward China's capital city, Beijing. Again, many people say the desert's spread is caused by global warming. But others say that the problem is overfarming and overgrazing.

While global warming could ruin some farmland, it might also open up new land for farming. Some scientists think that it may someday be possible to farm in northern Russia, Canada, Alaska, and Greenland. The weather in these areas could become mild and pleasant.

Only time will tell how global warming will change life for humans on Earth. For now, scientists are looking at the current weather. They are wondering whether what they see now is a sign of what the future may hold.

Chapter 4

Should Measures Be Taken to Fight Global Warming?

Some people want to take action against global warming now. Many of these people share the views of Gregg Easterbrook. Easterbrook is an editor for the *Atlantic Monthly*. "Greenhouse gases are an air pollution problem," Easterbrook writes. "The only reason runaway global warming seems unstoppable is that we have not yet tried to stop it."[7] Easterbrook's approach is to pass new laws. These laws would set greenhouse gas limits. Vehicles and factories would have to release fewer greenhouse gases into the air.

Other people are looking for better energy sources. They say humans should not depend on fossil fuels. Humans should stop burning fossil fuels. Then fewer greenhouse gases would be released into the air.

Reducing Greenhouse Gases

California has already passed new laws. California is a big state. It has the fifth-largest economy in the world. California gives off large amounts of greenhouse gas. Only eight other places give off more. Californians release about 12 tons (10.7t) of greenhouse gases into the air, per person, each year. In contrast, the United States gives off 19 tons (17t) of greenhouse gases per person every year. It is the largest emitter of greenhouse gases in the world.

California is taking steps to slow global warming. It is planting trees. Trees absorb carbon dioxide as they grow. California also encourages people to build solar houses. Solar houses can stay warm without burning any oil or gas. They get their energy from the Sun.

Protesters in Canada show their concern about global warming.

A solar-powered house in Norway does not need fossil fuels for energy.

New Laws

California also made new laws that affect cars and trucks. It requires them to give off less carbon dioxide. California had been releasing more greenhouse gas into the air every year. Lawmakers decided this had to stop. Instead, they wanted California to give off less gas every year. California's automakers do not think this is possible. They are taking the state of California to court. They hope that California will change its laws.

Some businesses, though, agree with the new laws. They find the laws help them save money. DuPont is giving off less greenhouse gas. It has reduced its emissions by 70 percent. And it has saved $2 billion. IBM reduced its emissions by 65 percent. It saved $791 million.

Reducing greenhouse gas emissions saves money because fossil fuels are expensive. If companies buy less, they save money. Some companies are making engines that burn fuel more efficiently. This means

A Carbon Footprint?

California and Iceland are examples of governments working to slow down global warming. But individual people are trying to help, too. They help by reducing their carbon footprints. A carbon footprint is a way to measure how much each person affects the environment.

Every person's carbon footprint is different. On the Internet, several Web sites have carbon footprint calculators. A calculator asks people questions. It keeps track of how a person's home is heated. It keeps track of electricity usage. It notes how each person gets to school or work. For example, walking to school does not leave a carbon footprint. Neither does riding a bicycle. But driving to school does.

Some people work at reducing their carbon footprints. They turn off lights that they are not using. They live in small homes that are easy to heat. They sometimes even build solar homes. They also drive small cars. A few drive hybrid cars, cars that run on electricity some of the time. They also try to buy food that is grown nearby. That way, the food has not been shipped across the country. Food that is shipped from far away must travel by truck, train, ship, or airplane.

Reducing one's carbon footprint may slow down global warming. At least, say its supporters, it cannot hurt.

that the engines can do more work with less fuel. That way fuel is not used up as quickly. And the company can buy less fuel. Other businesses have switched to cleaner forms of energy. Some have begun to use solar energy, for example.

Clean Energy

Clean energy is energy that is produced without giving off any air pollution. Fossil fuels are not a clean energy. Burning them releases pollutants into the air. Burning fossil fuels also releases carbon dioxide.

Several countries are racing to become the first ever to stop using fossil fuels. Right now Iceland is in the lead.

Iceland

About 50 years ago, Iceland converted its electric systems. It stopped using fossil fuels. Instead, it began using hydroelectric power. It also uses geothermal energy. Hydroelectric power is electricity. It is made using the power of flowing water. Geothermal energy is made using the natural heat of Earth. In some places, like Iceland, hot water or steam rises to the land's surface from deep within Earth. When this happens, hot springs form.

Iceland converted more than just its electric system. It also converted almost all of its heating systems. Very few homes in Iceland are heated by burning oil. Fewer than 3 percent are. Most are heated with geothermal heat. About 15 percent are heated

with electricity. But the electricity is made using hydropower.

Hydrogen Energy

Next Iceland turned to its buses. One option might have been to use electric power. However, Iceland decided to try a new form of energy. It decided to try hydrogen power. Humans can make hydrogen. All that is needed are water and electricity. Iceland has plenty of both. Hydrogen power is also clean energy. When vehicles run on hydrogen, only water vapor is given off.

In 2003 Iceland began converting to hydrogen power. It bought three hydrogen buses. It also built a hydrogen fueling station. The fueling station is like a gas station. But it sells hydrogen, not gasoline. The

Some of Iceland's buses, such as this one, run on hydrogen.

buses are very quiet. At first they seemed a little fragile. They could not always run on frosty days. But now the buses can run in temperatures down to -4°F (-20°C).

Clean Cars and Boats

In 2007 a few Icelanders began to drive hydrogen cars. They can fill their cars up at the hydrogen station. Then they can drive 100 miles (161km). When they run out of fuel, they can go another 18 miles (29km). That is because hydrogen cars have electric batteries, too. While the car runs on hydrogen, the battery charges up. When the car runs out of hydrogen, the battery can be used. It will not take the car very far. But it may be enough to get the car to a filling station.

Hydrogen cars, though, still cost about five times as much as gasoline-burning cars. In time, car companies believe they can bring the price down. In Iceland, however, people may be willing to buy expensive cars. They might do it to avoid buying

The Kyoto Protocol

Many countries are trying to work together to slow down global warming. These countries signed a treaty with each other. The treaty is called the Kyoto Protocol. A treaty is an agreement. The Kyoto Protocol is an agreement that countries will try to reduce their carbon footprints.

The Kyoto Protocol has been around since 1997. That is when it was first proposed. Some countries signed it right away. Others, such as the United States, have not signed it.

According to the Kyoto Protocol, each country has a target. But each country is in a different situation. So each country's target is different. Also, the terms of the agreement do not require each country to reduce its emissions. Instead, they can do other things. They can plant trees. They can give money to another country to help it reduce its emissions.

Many people disagree with the Kyoto Protocol. They think it is not fair because it has different rules for different countries. Others think that the Kyoto Protocol cannot help. They say that it does not call for deep enough cuts in emissions.

Melting ice floats in a bay near the Arctic Circle, one of many places affected by global warming.

gasoline. All of Iceland's gasoline is imported from other countries. It costs about eight dollars a gallon (two dollars a liter). That is almost three times the price of gasoline in the United States.

Testing a Hydrogen Ship

Next Iceland plans to convert its fishing fleet. But this will be hard. A boat cannot stop at a hydrogen station to fuel up. It would have to come back to shore to get fuel. Ships might have to carry extra hydrogen with them. Iceland is building a ship that will run on hydrogen. It will be a test ship. The ship will test how well the new fuel works at sea.

Not everyone thinks that using hydrogen power will slow down global warming. Hydrogen fuel systems give off water vapor. Water vapor, like carbon dioxide, is a greenhouse gas. On the other hand, water may not stay in the air very long. Carbon dioxide can stay in the air for years. Water may not. It may form clouds. Then it could fall as rain. Or it could become dew. Hydrogen technology is very new. Scientists are not yet sure how adding water vapor to the air could affect Earth's climate.

Likewise, no one is certain that humans will be able to slow down global warming. Small changes can make a difference to the world's climate. But small changes act by setting other changes in motion. It could be years before scientists know whether human efforts helped. How warm will Earth become? Only time will tell.

Notes

Introduction: Melting Glaciers

1. Quoted in Daniel Glick, "The Big Thaw," *National Geographic,* 2004. http://magma. nationalgeographic.com/ngm/0409/feature2/ index.html.

Chapter 3: What Will Be the Effects of Global Warming?

2. David Bromwich, "Antarctic Temperatures Disagree with Climate Model Predictions," Ohio State University press release, February 15, 2007. www.eurekalert.org/pub_releases/2007-02/osu-atd021207.php.
3. Bromwich, "Antarctic Temperatures Disagree with Climate Model Predictions."
4. Quoted in Andrew Darby, "Sentinels for a Lost World," *Sydney Morning Herald,* September 25, 2007. www.smh.com/au/news/environment/ sentinels-for-a-lost-world/2007/09/24/1190 486226019.html.
5. Quoted in Tom Kizzia, "Alaska Polar Bears Called Doomed," *Anchorage Daily News,* September 8,

2007. http://www.adn.com/news/alaska/wildlife/bears/polar_bears/story/9286663p-9200531c.html.

6. Quoted in Leslie Allen, "Will Tuvalu Disappear Beneath the Sea?" *Smithsonian Magazine,* August 2004. http://www.smithsonianmag.com/travel/tuvalu.html?c=y&page=2.

Chapter 4: Should Measures Be Taken to Fight Global Warming?

7. Gregg Easterbrook, "Some Convenient Truths," *Atlantic Monthly*, September 2006, p. 29.

Glossary

carbon dioxide: The gas that humans exhale. Carbon dioxide is also given off when fossil fuels are burned. It is a greenhouse gas.

climate: The weather in a place over a long period of time.

computer model: A model in a computer that shows something that could happen in the real world.

data: Information collected about a topic. Data usually includes measurements. For example, temperatures are a form of data.

fossil fuels: Fuels that formed over millions of years from the remains of plants and animals. Oil, coal, and gas are all fossil fuels.

global warming: Warming of the entire Earth. Scientists consider the Earth to be warming if its temperature rises one degree Celsius or more over a period of 100 years.

greenhouse effect: The ability that some gases have to trap heat inside Earth's atmosphere.

greenhouse gas: A gas that adds to the greenhouse effect.

ice age: A period of time when Earth's temperature drops and sheets of ice cover the land.

Industrial Revolution: The period of time when people began to use machines.

orbit: The movement of one object in space around another. For example, Earth orbits the Sun.

temperature: A measurement that shows how warm something is.

tilt: The slant of Earth's axis.

variable: Anything that may vary, or change.

Bibliography

Books

Laurie David and Cambria Gordon, *Down-to-Earth Guide to Global Warming.* London: Orchard Books, 2007. This book presents the point of view that people should try to stop global warming and gives ideas for things kids can do to reduce their carbon footprints.

Holly Fretwell, *The Sky's Not Falling! Why It's Okay to Chill About Global Warming.* Los Angeles: World Ahead, 2007. This book presents the point of view that global warming is not a threat and that people should do nothing about it.

Robyn Friend, *A Clean Sky: The Global Warming Story.* Marina del Rey, CA: Cascade Pass, 2007. This book discusses the various options that people are pursuing to slow down global warming, including using hydrogen energy.

Web Sites

Clean Air Kids (www.clean-air-kids.org.uk/air quality.html). A short history of air pollution, with a link to a page on global warming.

"Climate Change Kids' Site," U.S. Environmental Protection Agency (www.epa.gov/climatechange/kids/index.html). Includes animations of the carbon and water cycles, explains how people affect the environment, and includes sections on climate changes in history and how climate change works.

"Paleoclimatology: Explaining the Evidence," National Aeronautics and Space Administration (http://earthobservatory.nasa.gov/study/paleo climatology_intro). The beginning page of NASA's Web site on past climate change. Explains what scientists know about Earth's ice ages and how they know it.

Index

Picture Credits

About the Author

Bonnie Juettner is a writer and editor of children's reference books and educational videos. She is also a mother of two. She is especially interested in global warming because of its effects on her former home state, Alaska.